Copyright © 2024 Kay Mosser.

All rights reserved. No part of this book may be used or reproduced by any means, graphic, electronic, or mechanical, including photocopying, recording, taping or by any information storage retrieval system without the written permission of the author except in the case of brief quotations embodied in critical articles and reviews.

Archway Publishing books may be ordered through booksellers or by contacting:

Archway Publishing
1663 Liberty Drive
Bloomington, IN 47403
www.archwaypublishing.com
844-669-3957

Because of the dynamic nature of the Internet, any web addresses or links contained in this book may have changed since publication and may no longer be valid. The views expressed in this work are solely those of the author and do not necessarily reflect the views of the publisher, and the publisher hereby disclaims any responsibility for them.

Any people depicted in stock imagery provided by Getty Images are models, and such images are being used for illustrative purposes only. Certain stock imagery © Getty Images.

ISBN: 978-1-6657-5372-2 (sc)
ISBN: 978-1-6657-5371-5 (hc)
ISBN: 978-1-6657-5370-8 (e)

Print information available on the last page.

Archway Publishing rev. date: 04/19/2024

Chapter 1
What was I thinking?

On a cool, spring morning, after all the children had gone to school, I busied myself in the kitchen with the aftermath of breakfast time. I heard the phone ring and answered it. It was an old friend of mine, Sarah Jean. She told me she called to ask a favor of me—well, a favor of my children.

Sara Jean lived on a farm and had a petting zoo. It featured a variety of animals that she would take to the county fair and other events. The petting zoo included pygmy goats. It just so happened that one of her nannies – mama goats – had given birth to triplets!

Just imagine that: three, tiny baby goats at the same time!

This was a problem. The nanny could only feed *two* of the kids, or baby goats. This meant that the extra kid would need to be bottle-fed.

Sarah knew from experience that my kids were very good with animals and that they could bottle-feed this little pygmy kid until it got old enough to go back to Sarah Jean and her petting zoo.

We chatted for a few more minutes on the phone while I thought about it, but I told her, "No." I knew my children would get too attached to it—they would NEVER let the goat go back home. There would be tears and begging if I even tried. Why would I want to cause my children the pain of giving up a goat they raised?

So, if I decided to let the children take care of the goat, I would just have to buy it from her.

When my children got home from school, I explained to them what Sarah Jean and I had talked about. I told them we'd head to the farm before it got dark.

Now, if I had really been thinking this through, if I had an ounce of sense in me, I would NOT have taken two little girls with me to see a furry, cute, little pygmy goat. Where, oh where, was my common sense? Did I really think I would come home empty-handed after this little adventure? So much for clear thinking!

We arrived at the farm, and my little girls were extremely anxious to take on this *work project*. At the back door to my friend's kitchen, Sarah Jean happily welcomed us in.

Immediately, from somewhere under a cabinet, leaped out a small, precious, black fur-covered, cuddly pygmy goat.

By Rachel Sparinga, Friend of Kay Mosser

MY FIRST RED FLAG! The goat was in the house and already considered herself a member of the family. She rushed out to greet my girls, and they quickly began giggling and hugging her.

With a closer eye, I realized that this pygmy kid was *smaller* than our three-legged cat Moe! Her coat was so soft and shiny. A small, white patch adorned her face. How cute was that? She was so small that each hoof was the size of a nickel.

If she stood still – and that's a BIG 'if' – you would think she was a stuffed animal. All in all, she was an adorably fuzzy package of total cuteness.

Who could resist? Not us! Fifty dollars *jumped* out of my wallet, and soon my two little girls and I were on our way home with that little kid. I always kept a baby blanket in my car for those cool summer evenings, so we wrapped up that pygmy baby that we already loved so very much.

But first things first, she needed a name. After much debate and consideration, my children decided to call this baby goat Clara Jean, after my friend Sarah Jean who sold this cute animal to us.

Chapter 2
Clara Jean Runs the House

Feeding Clara Jean began shortly after we arrived home. Although my children wanted Clara Jean to live in their bedrooms and sleep in their beds, I only gave in as far as keeping her on the back porch.

This would keep her protected and accessible, not to mention keeping the kids' rooms *clean*. The little girls found a couple of small baby bottles and patiently took turns warming the milk and then feeding Clara Jean.

By Granddaughter, age 7

She loved every minute of this attention and companionship. Naturally, Clara Jean imprinted on the little girls and followed them *everywhere*. This was delightful for everyone! However, the first Sunday after we brought her home, we didn't think our usual routine of going to church and leaving Clara Jean at home was a bad thing.

Well, Clara Jean felt like we deserted her! Abandoned her! Left her alone for the rest of her life!

At least, I *think* that this was her story.

Well, when we arrived home several hours later, we could tell Clara Jean was ticked. She was mad. She was insulted. She went on a hunger strike! For a day or two, the stubborn little thing wouldn't eat, and my poor little girls fretted and worried!

That didn't last long, and things got back to normal. Clara Jean received excellent care, helping her grow. If only it had helped her to mature as well.

Every time the kitchen door opened, a little black flash bolted through it. She wanted in the house. After all, she was sure that she was a person, too.

As fast as she could, she ran through the house, jumping and hopping on the furniture and the beds, with all my children chasing close behind her.

Each adventure like this was a funny thing to watch, especially if you weren't the children's mother. Everyone was overjoyed and full of energy and laughter. For a while, I think this is exactly how everyone got their daily exercise, including me! Clara Jean didn't mind all the noise, laughter, and chasing. It's probably what goats like best!

Chapter 3
She loved being chased!

By Kay Mosser, Author

Soon, I realized that the carpets needed cleaning. As you could imagine, between several children and a certain pygmy goat, the floor wasn't very stain-free anymore.

I called my typical carpet cleaners, and on the day that they arrived, I left to take care of a quick errand. I trusted them well and knew they could work without my supervision.

But when I came home, one of the workers met me at the door and excitedly related this story:

"Mrs. Mosser, we really tried hard, but...well...that little black goat somehow squeezed in as we were coming and going, right where we had the hose in the doorway."

My eyes got big as the carpet cleaning employee continued.

"She ran from room to room, jumping all over your furniture, but we just couldn't catch her. She's so fast!"

I waited, thinking something awful was coming.

"It took us quite a while to herd her toward the door. I'm so sorry, but I honestly think that she *liked* being chased!" A smile fell upon my face. Yes. That would be a big yes. She LOVED being chased.

Chapter 4
Beautified

By Kay Mosser, Author

As Clara Jean continued to grow, my daughter Miriam decided to play beauty shop with the goat. With her sister Winona's help, they gave Clara Jean's coat a shampoo, blow dry, and thorough brushing.

My, how she did *shine*! Her little hooves and budding horns were manicured and painted with sparkly purple nail polish. Could she have been more adorable? Clara Jean knew the answer to that: she pranced all around.

It even looked like she was showing off a bit, like she knew she was the most gorgeous of goats! I wish I had seen this coming, but giving Clara Jean an attitude of airs about her beautiful little hooves later proved to be the cause of some very negative outcomes.

Chapter 5
A Goat Wants to Go to School

Getting the kids on the bus in the morning soon became a very difficult daily event. Clara Jean would follow my husband Frank and our children down the road each morning to wait for the bus. When the bus arrived, Clara Jean would actually try to get on it with her playmates!

Frank was having a tough time trying to restrain her from going to school, too. (Didn't Clara Jean hear what happened to Mary's Little Lamb when she tried to go to school? The teacher put her out.) Frank would stomp back to the house very frustrated, always with the same story.

I know that I was only thinking my frustrations aloud when I said, "Well, why don't you let her? Maybe she'll get off the bus at the next bus stop!" So much for wishing...

By Granddaughter, age 10

Chapter 6
The Circus Goat

Then came the cold spring weather. Playing outside was a great idea, but Clara Jean began to shiver. Of course, my children had compassion for her and simply brought her back into the house until they could figure out how to warm her up.

In my mind, I already had the solution: I would cut the sleeve out of an old red sweater and make her a coat. And it worked! The sweater sleeve covered her whole body except for where I had cut holes in the bottom for her legs to go through. Clara Jean wore her sweater proudly and her followers went outside again.

However, it wasn't long before my children came back into the house, laughing their heads off and begging me to come outside and see what Clara Jean could do. I joined the small circle of kids surrounding Clara Jean outside in the backyard and watched her perform an amazing trick. And I thought that the scene was hilarious, too! You see, the sweater tickled her back legs.

She didn't like that feeling, so she put her head down, lifted her two rear legs, and walked on her front feet, just like a trained circus animal! Her audience applauded and just loved her antics! One point for the goat!

By Grandson, age 7

Chapter 7

Here Comes Trouble (or Beauty and the Poop)

But it wasn't always fun and games.

Oh, that Clara Jean. What started as a tiny, innocent-looking pygmy baby turned into a goat teenager that got into more trouble than we could imagine! And not everyone thought she was funny, *especially* when she got into trouble.

She developed a fondness for jumping on top of automobile hoods, but even worse than that was she preferred the really shiny ones! You know, the ones that were just washed, dried, and waxed? Those were her favorites! She found it fun to jump on the roof and slide down the windshield. If you were a goat, this would be the highlight of your day. If you were sitting inside that shiny car when someone's goat did that to your automobile, you wouldn't be too happy.

As it happened, some of my husband Frank's customers fell into the "not too happy" category. We had a few complaints, usually from the husbands, even though their wives were mostly giggles and comments of "How cute!"

One of those "not too happy" gentlemen pulled up to the back of our home in a gray Cadillac to inquire about a vehicle my husband Frank had for sale. You know what happened next: that little, black, fuzzy, manicured goat promptly jumped up on his hood. He was not amused! It seemed that Clara enjoyed the chase *and* the attention she got from running up and down on cars. Remember: the shinier, the better!

Adding to this sequence of bad behavior, it was on another bright and beautiful day when our oldest son Ward had just washed and polished his classic hotrod, a 1973 Oldsmobile Omega. He had recently had it painted bright red, and he was so proud of his beautiful car. It was *really* shiny, and Clara Jean just couldn't resist.

She really did it that day!

The exact moment Ward finished cleaning the car, he went into the house to freshen up so he could go out that night. While he was preoccupied inside the house, Clara Jean jumped up on his newly-painted hood, leaving evidence of her in the form of little, muddy footprints.

As if that wasn't enough, she also jumped up on the roof of his car and slid down the windshield, leaving slide marks from her hooves.

To top it off, little Clara Jean left little Clara Jean droppings on his hood... and a sizable Goat Poop Ornament on the middle of the car hood!

By Kay Mosser, Author

When Ward came out of the house and saw his car, he was *livid*. I knew he wanted to get rid of her at once, but he maintained enough control to simply rip out of the driveway on his way to the nearest car wash.

It just so happened that on his way to the car wash, another car pulled out in front of Ward. He swerved to avoid the car, but he crashed into the guardrail. Fortunately for our family, Ward was unhurt as the accident wasn't on the driver's side. Unfortunately for Ward, his hot rod was totaled.

And all because of a little black pygmy goat named Clara Jean.

Several negative points for the goat.

One of Frank's employees drove his own classic car to work. The only disastrous mistake that he made around Clara Jean was to leave his windows down that warm day.

Of course, this pygmy goat was the self-appointed parking lot attendant on duty. In her tiny, devious head, she made such evil plans. She waited until Frank's worker was occupied inside the garage before jumping into the window and tearing out the headliner of that car.

The list of people who had negative feelings toward Clara Jean was growing by the day—or, should I say, by the car!

Chapter 8

Is She a Goat or a People?

How many more negative points would Clara Jean rack up before it was too much?

Summer came and hot weather returned. My sister Lelah, who lived close by, had a nice big swimming pool which she permitted my kids to use freely. On one sweltering day, my kids asked permission to go to Aunt Lelah's for a swim. They quickly changed to swimsuits and proceeded through the yard toward her home. Can you guess who followed them? Well, none other than Clara Jean, hot on their trail and arriving only slightly behind them at the swimming pool.

Everyone ran and jumped into the pool. Following their lead (as usual), Clara Jean also ran at her top speed and jumped into the pool. Guess what? She could swim! The kids were so surprised and utterly delighted to have Clara Jean splashing in the water with them.

The children informed me of Clara Jean's latest antics once they returned home from their swimming trip. Though she entertained them, they did worry and begged, "Mom, *please* don't tell Aunt Lelah that Clara Jean was swimming in her pool!"

By Kay Mosser, Author

As summer progressed, not-so-little Clara Jean's horns were growing larger, and she started to butt things.

A little head-butt can mean "I love you" or "Let's play!" in goat language. Sometimes, a goat will just head-butt something like a ball or a bucket to see what happens. Of course, when the goat realizes the ball rolls after head-butting it, they now see it as new entertainment.

Chapter 9
This Baaaaad Goat

Clara Jean's playful little butts and pushes seemed harmless until one day when she butted Miriam's arm so hard that she bruised it. I would *not* accept this behavior – goat or not – especially with my younger kids. Yet, we realized that Clara Jean couldn't stop being a goat any more than we could stop being humans...*even if she did consider herself to be a person.*

At this point, our family had to talk about Clara Jean and all the trouble she was getting into and causing. It was decided that we would have to place her in a pen.

Because we no longer had an enclosure suitable for such a creature, our very busy teenage son Ward, anxious to be about his business after work and school, was *not* happy when he was tasked to build her a pen.

After all, there had been the episode with his beautiful, red car. In his words, "Mom, there's bad blood between me and Clara."

But dutiful and obedient, Ward used whatever materials he could find in the used lumber pile and built a small enclosure with metal posts surrounded by 3-foot-high chicken wire fence. It wasn't too shabby, and it seemed like a perfect place for her. She would still be able to see and be close to us, but not so close that she could cause problems.

The next morning, Clara Jean was placed in her new, enclosed home with its large fence. From the moment in which she was placed there, she commenced a "dying little goat" act, something we were much too familiar with to believe.

Oh, she tried to convince us with her bleating cries until one of her loved ones would feel sorry enough for her to do exactly what she wanted: break down her fence to let her escape. As for the accommodations, I don't believe that she ever even acknowledged her fine home. All she did was pace back and forth and around the gate, head-butting the wire repeatedly with her sparkly, purple horns. The butting and baaing were constant and incessant.

For three days, Clara was determined to find her own way out, and within a few weeks she was able to do just that: the 3-foot fencing was no longer sufficient to hold her as soon as she learned she could jump.

Chapter 10
Ward vs. Clara Jean

This was a *real* problem. Now, Ward was quite upset and really didn't want to waste time building a new enclosure for this *baaaaad* goat.

Discouraged and distraught, Ward slunk to his room and sat down on his bed for only a moment when he spied his 5-pound ankle weights on the floor.

"Imagine," he said, "watching Clara Jean try to jump with an ankle weight around her belly!"

Ward thought that he had her now, and he honestly believed that he had outsmarted her this time. He was confident that he had won this round against her.

Why, if Ward could use those weights to perfect his own amazing jumping abilities, why wouldn't he think that it would give the same magical jumping powers to Clara Jean?

By Granddaughter, age 7

The very next day found Ward with ankle weights in hand, running up to the enclosure to have a little one-on-one time with Clara Jean. He promptly fastened the weights around the belly of this little creature—amazingly, they fit well enough. Problem solved! At least, that's what he thought.

Clara Jean was just a little bit smarter than that. She used the ankle weight as her daily exercise. Oh, sure, Ward thought it was grand to watch the ornery goat stay grounded, not even able to jump one foot off the ground.

But a funny thing happens when you exercise with weights day in and day out: Clara Jean appeared to be getting stronger. Soon, she looked like a bodybuilding goat with rippling muscles.

During this same Ward vs. Clara Jean debacle, my other children would hide on the back porch and peek at her. If Clara Jean caught them watching her, she would immediately fall back into the desperate "dying little goat" act.

Well, she *was* extremely angry with her "supposed" family. She felt <u>insulted</u>. How could that tall boy Ward do this thing to her? Clara Jean's little black eyes held rage and fire. Determined not to be detained, Clara Jean fought harder.

She practiced and practiced and practiced and perfected her jumping with that ankle weight on her belly. Nothing, no nothing, was going to stop her!

Chapter 11
Reed's "Little Black Demon"

So, we held another family council. Everyone (except for Ward) decided that the ankle weights were too much strain on poor, little, "dying" Clara Jean. Surely her bleating and *Baaaa*-ing meant she was exhausting herself. All after school exercise sessions with Ward were cancelled. Little did we know that Clara Jean's weighty determination and practice had already paid off. Clara Jean discovered that she could *easily* jump the fence, and jump it she did.

You can guess what happened next.

My husband Frank sat down to explain to our teenage son Ward just how necessary it had become to build a *super* pen to keep that darned goat inside it. Really, how hard could it be to contain a cute, little, black pygmy goat?

More serious than getting his goat-poop car washed off that fateful night, Ward took this task seriously. He dug holes, installed heavy wooden posts, lined the bottom of the fence with woven wire, and topped it off with chicken wire, going up seven feet in height. We all anticipated the day Ward finished so we could place Little Miss Clara Jean in her new super pen. At first, she gave the "dying little goal" act, but we didn't fall for it.

Then, she tried the "desperate little goat" act, in which she cried louder. (It even looked like fake tears adorned her furry cheeks!) When that proved unsuccessful, she crossed her face with a sour look and showed us her super jumping abilities.

The first time, she got up to almost five feet in the air! Though she didn't reach the top after several attempts, and falling quite violently to the ground each time, Clara Jean decided to hurl her little body at the fence. The trauma of watching her was too much. The family (again, except for Ward) decided that fortifying the enclosure would lead to her harming herself, but what to do?

Since Clara Jean was immensely disturbed by being fenced in, another alternative was needed. This time, Frank seemed to have the best solution. He thought that he could use an old car axle as a stake pounded into the ground with a swiveling anchor on the end to tie to Clara Jean's neck. The swivel part would give Clara Jean enough freedom while ensuring she didn't get tangled up in the chain. The plan seemed viable. It *should* work. Now, it was Frank's turn to try to control "The Little Black Demon," as our youngest child Reed had begun to call her.

After procuring all the necessary items, Frank went to the uppermost part of our yard and planted the stake firmly in the hard, clay soil. Next, he attached the swivel and chain to the stake.

By this time, we all knew the drill: hide behind the banisters of the back porch and watch what happened! Gingerly, Frank attached little, black, furry Clara Jean to the chain and ran as fast as he could as she chased him toward the house.

But when she got to the end of her chain, it jerked her back slightly, and that only served to make her madder! She tried the chain from all different angles to see how far she could pull it. Over the course of a few days, we believed that she would get used to the chain, give up, and settle down.

As usual, Clara Jean's dark, little mind worked overtime until she developed a plan. She would run and pull, run and pull, *run and pull!*

She continued endlessly until we became afraid that she was going to hurt herself again in her determined efforts.

Chapter 12
And the Impossible Happened

Back to the family discussions again. As we talked at length about what we could possibly do now, Frank came up with another great plan. Frank had always loved bungee stretchers. In fact, he used them for everything, so why not a goat?

He attached several bungee stretchers together like a long rope and then attached that rope to the end of the chain so that Clara Jean wouldn't get jerked.

Wow!

What an amazing idea!

We couldn't wait to see it in action!

Like all the previous times, we lined up in the yard to get a better look at the action. Clara Jean knew we were there. She ran toward the house to test the feel of the chain and bungee cords together. She went back toward the stake and ran another direction, back to the stake and yet another direction, over and over until she felt satisfied about the strength of the chain and the stretchers.

She defiantly glared at us, slowly walked the chain to the farthest part of the yard and turned to face us. With those black-beaded eyes, she uttered a loud triumphant "BAA!" and pawed the ground with her hooves. She dropped her head and charged as fast as she could until she almost reached us.

Now the bungee stretchers were stretched as far as they could possibly stretch. With riveted attention, we watched in horror, mouths gaping open, as we heard a popping sound: it was the link on Clara's collar snapping! To our amazement, she was airborne!

By Granddaughter, age 12

Clara Jean was *flying*!

Our goat was FLYING, like a tiny black torpedo!

She flew high up into the air, back towards the woods, and into the trees... out of sight. The very last thing that we heard was a high-pitched "BAA!"

What just happened? How could this be? What do we do now? We quickly spread out in different directions. The search began. We couldn't imagine her being out there by herself. Frank went left, I went to the right, and four kids scattered between us.

We called her name and searched around every bush and tree as we slowly ambled through the woods. Exhaustion was beginning to take hold of us when we heard Miriam call, "Over here! Quick, over here!" Satisfied, she smiled and pointed down at her feet. There upon the ground, blending with the decaying leaves, lay Clara Jean droppings!

Delight was rampant among us! Clara Jean was alive and moving! The tree was three-tenths of a mile from the house.

Miriam's discovery prompted more careful examination of the ground where we had already been looking.

Winona was the next to find a little pile of "treasure" behind a large oak tree. This tree was fifty feet from the first tree. Also, at the base of this tree trunk, the soft dirt held little, pointed hoof prints. A pattern was emerging. It almost appeared that Clara Jean had been watching our frantic searching from behind different trees. Interesting to us was the fact that the little goat who couldn't stop complaining could be quiet if she wanted to!

Did she stand behind a tree, coldly glaring at us and smiling her evil goat smile as she watched us run back and forth looking for her? How could she worry us so much?

We were the family who loved her. But we were also the family that confined her. This was against her principals. After all, Clara Jean was a person, wasn't she? Did she run away because she wanted more freedom than we could give her? Knowing her, I could imagine what the sassy, little, black thing was doing!

By Kay Mosser, Author

But the real question was, what was *she* thinking?

In her anger, was she feeling vengeful?

Did she want to cause us as much distress and anxiety as possible?

Did she want those kids to worry and fret about her?

Could she be that *devious*, after all the love and care my children had given her?

In some ways, I didn't want to know how Clara Jean's mind worked! Perhaps we really didn't want to find out. In our anxiety and desperate search, we wondered where she went.

Have *YOU* seen a little black goat in your yard lately?

(Turn Page)

EPILOGUE

A few months later:

While on route to a public swimming pool, one of the kids from the back of the station wagon excitedly yelled, "Look, Mom! Out in that field! Do you see that little black goat?" Sure enough, there was a little, black pygmy goat among a herd of white dairy goats. We noticed that a very high fence had been installed around the field.

We don't know for sure, but we could swear that we saw a little white spot on its face. At this point, one of the little girls wanted to go have a closer look.

I thought for about five seconds and decided that maybe it wasn't a good idea...for the little goat.

After all, if this goat was Clara Jean, she looked quite content among her own people. I thought that if this was the case, we shouldn't disturb her peace and tranquility. After noting her position in the center of the herd, I was pretty convinced that it was indeed Clara Jean. She elevated herself to the position of Queen Clara Jean, and was keeping a watchful eye on her subjects.

With those thoughts in mind, none of us thought it necessary to investigate further. Some of us thought that maybe she relocated herself to this farm and that the farmer was driven to install a fence worthy of a penitentiary to keep that demonic little goat in! But no one really knows for sure.

It's possible that we'll hear the rest of her story at some point in time!

Printed in the USA
CPSIA information can be obtained
at www.ICGtesting.com
LVHW060004230524
780683LV00003B/96